IMAGES OF ENGLAND

WEYMOUTH
AND PORTLAND

IMAGES OF ENGLAND

WEYMOUTH AND PORTLAND

GEOFF PRITCHARD AND ANDY HUTCHINGS

Frontispiece: The Jubilee Clock, Weymouth Esplanade prior to the widening of the promenade in 1922.

First published in 2004 by Tempus Publishing
Reprinted 2005, 2008

Reprinted in 2011 by
The History Press,
The Mill, Brimscombe Port,
Stroud, Gloucestershire, GL5 2QG
www.thehistorypress.co.uk

Reprinted in 2016

© Geoff Pritchard and Andy Hutchings, 2011

The right of Geoff Pritchard and Andy Hutchings to be identified as the Authors of this work has been asserted in accordance with the Copyrights, Designs and Patents Act 1988.

All rights reserved. No part of this book may be reprinted or reproduced or utilised in any form or by any electronic, mechanical or other means, now known or hereafter invented, including photocopying and recording, or in any information storage or retrieval system, without the permission in writing from the Publishers.

British Library Cataloguing in Publication Data.
A catalogue record for this book is available from the British Library.

ISBN 978 0 7524 3066 9

Typesetting and origination by
Tempus Publishing.
Printed and bound in England.

Contents

	Acknowledgements	6
	About the Authors	6
	Introduction	7
one	Around Weymouth	9
two	Around Portland	47
three	The Surrounding Districts	79
four	Events	95
five	Ships and Transport	113

Acknowledgements

The authors wish to thank all those persons who have assisted them in the compilation of this book: Maureen Attwooll; Stuart Morris; Brian Jackson; David Lane; Bill Macey; Richard Clammer; the late Doug Hollings; Colin Pomeroy; Rodney Alcock; Richard Samways; Jenny; the staff of Weymouth Central Library and Geoff's wife Marcia for her constructive comments and filling in the gaps in our knowledge on the finer points of IT. The Authors wish to record their appreciation of the encouragement given by the late Geoffrey Poole (1925-2016), lecturer, geomorphologist, local historian and campaigner.

We have made every possible attempt to trace copyright, and would like to apologise to anyone we may have inadvertently left out of these acknowledgements.

A donation is being made from the sale of each book to the Joseph Weld and Trimar Hospices, Dorchester.

About the Authors

Geoff Pritchard has lived in Weymouth since a very early age and was educated at Weymouth Grammar School and Bournemouth College of Technology. His career in local government spanned 37 years until his retirement in 2003 as Senior Committe Administrator. Since then he has been involved in local history research.

Andy Hutchings was born in Weymouth and served for 24 years as a Weymouth and Portland Borough Councillor. An Honorary Alderman of the Borough, he now serves on a number of public bodies and is a volunteer member of the Weymouth to Bristol Rail Partnership. He is an avid collector of Edwin Seward postcards.

They are the joint authors of two books on Edwin Seward postcards and are regular contributors to the local press on local history.

A hive of activity from around 1909 which epitomises the activities of the Great Western shipping services from Weymouth. The 'Jersey Boat' has arrived and the former Whitland and Cardigan saddle tank locomotive used on the Quay Tramway would shortly couple up to the boat train. Horse-drawn transport was available for those not catching the train and ferrymen would row customers across to the Nothe. It is difficult to imagine from this picture that the social revolution, which would begin with the First World War, was not far off!

Introduction

The origin of this book came from a collection of postcards of Weymouth and the surrounding area started by Andy Hutchings' maternal grandmother, who moved from London to Weymouth in the 1960s. On her death the collection passed to Andy's mother who in turn passed it on to Andy. He noticed the high quality of the cards published by Edwin Seward and began to collect cards of Weymouth and district by this postcard publisher. The current collection amounts to approximately 1,600 cards.

Edwin Henry Seward was born on 9 August 1877 at No. 15 Mount Place, Southampton. His father was Edwin Elswood Seward, a coach painter originally from Ilminster, Somerset, and his mother Henrietta Rosalina Frederica Cook. The couple married in Southampton in December 1874 and their first child, a daughter, Gassine, was born in 1876, followed by Edwin Henry a year later. By 1881, the family had moved to Ryde on the Isle of Wight where their third child, Christina, was born in 1882. A year later the family moved again, this time to Weymouth, living at No. 15 Upway Street. Here, Edwin Henry's younger brothers, Herbert and William, were born in 1884 and 1886.

The move to Weymouth reunited Edwin's father with his younger brother Alfred who was a coachbuilder. Alfred already had a thriving coach-building business in Crescent Street. The two brothers, and later two of their sons, ran the firm for many years.

Young Edwin Henry, however, had no interest in joining the family firm – from an early age his passion was photography. He first found employment at Cummings Photographic Studios in St Mary Street, Weymouth, but later moved away for a while working in Leicester and Norwich. By 1901, at the age of twenty-four, he had moved to Bath, the census showing him living there as a boarder in a lodging house. His occupation was given as a photographic printer and it is probable that he was employed by The Milsom Photographic Company in Bath, who took his portrait photograph, seen overleaf.

Edwin Seward (1877-1954).

In 1907, Edwin returned to Weymouth and opened his own photographic studio at No. 13 Turton Street, renting the first floor of the property owned by the Weymouth Soda Water Company. His early work concentrated on scenes of historic interest in Weymouth and the county, establishing him as a photographer of some note in the town. He remained a bachelor until 1911, when he married Ellen Humphries in St Michael's Parish Church, Bath.

Over the following thirty years Edwin's photographic business continued to flourish. His Melcombe Series of postcards proved highly successful with huge sales. Popular too were his photographs of warships in Portland Harbour – mostly ships of the Royal Navy, but also a number of foreign vessels. Some illustrations in pre-war editions of *Jane's Fighting Ships* have a 'Seward, Weymouth' credit.

For relaxation, Edwin enjoyed hunting, regularly following the foxhounds on foot and going hare coursing and badger and otter hunting. However, his camera was never far from him and hunting scenes were an important part of his work.

In April 1929, Edwin and Ellen moved to No. 5 York Buildings on the Esplanade, where they lived until Edwin's death on 16 June 1954 after a brief illness.

Dorset Postcard Club, of which Andy is a member, was approached by Tempus Publishing to see whether any of its members would be prepared to assemble a collection of postcards from this region. Andy's collection seemed ideal and he asked his friend Geoff Pritchard who had a great interest and knowledge of local history if he would write the captions.

Edwin Henry Seward's legacy is a pictorial history of Weymouth and rural Dorset in the first half of the twentieth century, which survives through his postcards and photographs for us all to enjoy.

Geoff Pritchard and Andy Hutchings
July 2004

one
Around Weymouth

We start at the turn of the twentieth century and what more appropriate form of transport than a horse-drawn carriage waiting outside St John's Church, Weymouth, on a winter's day.

This Coronation Arch of 1911 commemorating the Coronation of King George V and Queen Mary was constructed on the Esplanade near its junction with King Street. It welcomed visitors to the Royal Counties Agricultural Show held off Dorchester Road at Lodmoor from 13-16 June that year. New decorations were then added to display sentiments more appropriate to the Coronation on Thursday 22 June. The sender of the card posted on 1 July lamented the wet weather that had had a detrimental effect on the roads and had prevented her from visiting the recipient, who lived in Blandford.

The Royal Hotel was a popular venue for events such as civic banquets and society dinners. Here it is seen decorated ready for such an occasion in the early years of the twentieth century. The hanging baskets would not look out of place in today's Weymouth in Bloom contest.

This view shows two of Weymouth's leading hotels, the Gloucester and the Royal. The original Gloucester Lodge was extended in 1862 and again in 1927 and the Royal, built in 1897, had replaced an earlier, smaller structure.

Left: This octagonal bathing machine is reputed to be the one used by King George III on his first visit to Weymouth in 1789. Notice the Royal crest at the top. Eventually there were three types of bathing machine in use on the beach – the octagonal type shown here, individual machines of a later design and large saloons.

Below: The Pier Bandstand when new in 1939. This became a popular open-air venue for dancing, roller-skating, bathing beauty contests and professional wrestling. However, problems were often experienced during wet weather, as the arena had no roof. The front elevation was extended in 1958 but more recent alterations have restored something of its original appearance. The condition of the pier structure deteriorated and it was demolished by explosives in 1986, the detonator being activated by the winner of a competition!

A view of the Esplanade along Brunswick Terrace showing the bandstand that stood there from 1907 to 1938. A small crowd is being entertained by a band concert but others stroll past, appearing to be rather uninterested. Hedges occupy the space now taken up with raised flowerbeds, and the small white stones connected by chains show the boundary of the Esplanade.

Donkey rides on the sands were, until very recently, a popular attraction for children. The sender of the card comments 'still the same old donkeys here'. The concession was operated by the Downton family from Victorian times until the 1990s and is missed by many people.

Above: A crowded beach on a sunny day in 1909. The van to the right of the Jubilee Clock appears to be part of a beach mission, an event that was very common at seaside resorts. The advertisement on the wall of No. 1 Royal Crescent is for G. Bryer Ash, a well-known local coal merchant.

Left: Two ladies pose for the camera on the shingle beach opposite the Hotel Burdon. One does not envy the lady who has to push the heavy bath chair along the beach.

A peaceful scene looking across the bay. The produce available on the stall looks interesting and includes bottled beer and bananas. The original Pavilion Theatre of 1908 stands proudly in the background.

A view showing the various types of bathing machines referred to earlier. The largest ones are the saloons and a regulation distance had to be kept between male and female saloons, although mixed bathing had been allowed by the time they were removed at the start of the Second World War.

It had snowed heavily and Edwin Seward was there to record the scene. The building at the end of Grosvenor Place was Tilley's cycle shop. This firm went on to be one of the leading motor agents in Weymouth and in 1907 built the County Garage in Victoria Street and further premises in Dorchester.

Building sandcastles has always been a favourite pastime on the beach. For many years competitions were held to find the best castle. These were sponsored by a number of commercial firms including Bovril and this photograph shows one such competition in progress.

The sender does not record if this was the winning entry in the sandcastle competition of 1909 but it certainly deserves to be so.

This picture of the Esplanade shows the dawn of the motor age. Horse-taxis still wait at a rank but one or two cars can be seen. The lack of motor transport has enabled sailors to walk down the middle of the road without fear of being run over.

Weymouth Esplanade showing a very rough sea in 1923. The only person about appears to be Seward himself. Oddly enough the writer of the card says 'weather fair'!

A snowy day showing the other end of the promenade looking towards St John's Church with the promise of more snow to come. A cab and a few lonely walkers brave the elements.

The Esplanade in 1921. To the west of the gable advertising the Dorothy Restaurant can be seen Stuckey's Bank of 1883. This was converted to public conveniences in the 1950s and must surely now be one of the most elaborate buildings for this purpose seen anywhere. In 2016 this has been offered for sale.

The Hotel Burdon, Victoria Terrace built in 1855. This was one of the largest hotels in Weymouth and was the meeting place for many local organisations. It is now called the Hotel Prince Regent and has recently undergone refurbishment. In this postcard a cycling policeman passes the hotel where the hotel bus is parked outside. The building is now owned by Daish, the national holiday company.

The helter-skelter shown here in 1923 had just recently been moved from an area north of Westham Bridge. It proved to be a popular attraction before the Second World War. Notice the absence of railings on the Esplanade which today would no doubt keep compensation lawyers busy!

The weather was not always fine in Weymouth and on this breezy day the beach attendants are putting out or taking in the gangways that lead to the bathing machines. The occupants of the beach are huddled on to a small strip of sand.

Right: The Memorial to Weymouth residents killed in the First World War was unveiled in 1921. Unfortunately ten years later the stonework was eroding. The names of the Fallen, together with the addition of many names previously omitted were etched on bronze plaques added to each face of the monument in 1932. Second World War casualties were commemorated on a town War Memorial in St Mary's Church dedicated in 1950, and these names were finally added to new plaques at the base of the memorial in 1997.

Below: By 1932, the date of this photograph, although the bathing machines are still in existence, the Esplanade has changed considerably in appearance. It has been widened and traffic islands have been installed. A cyclist appears to be crossing at the King Street junction.

A small boy walks proudly along the Promenade carrying his model yacht in 1937. Despite the attractions of the sands the sender of the postcard comments 'the stores here do not amount to much – there are better ones in Yeovil'.

By the summer of 1939 the motorcar had become a popular form of transport. Parking was allowed on the seafront and many motorists took advantage of this. The saloon bathing huts still existed but would be removed on the outbreak of war. The Pier Bandstand, seen in the background, was newly opened.

Another popular facility was the fleet of beach canoes and floats, operated for many years by Edgar Wallis, who later became a member of the Borough Council and Mayor of Weymouth in 1960. He was also a local hotelier.

This postcard is entitled 'Beachcombers at Weymouth', although they all appear to be standing on the Promenade. Beachcombing in its true sense would have put them at severe risk!

Horse-buses were a common feature around Weymouth at the turn of the century. A number, including one belonging to G.E. Bugler of Rodwell Mews, wait at the Statue in 1907. Mr Bugler was shortly to turn his attention to operating motor taxis and, later, charabancs. A poster advertises the Weymouth Regatta, and another St Paul's Church Garden fête.

This shows an uninterrupted view of Royal Terrace before the encroachment of shop fronts at ground-floor level. This terrace was developed from around 1815. One building at the left end of the terrace was demolished in 1929 for the widening of the junction with Westham Road.

This photograph of the Alexandra Gardens was taken between 1904, when the thatched shelters were built, and 1913 when the Kursaal was constructed. This was a glass structure added to the original bandstand that provided protection from the weather for the audiences who came to hear the bands which played.

The Kursaal survived until 1924, when the Alexandra Gardens Concert Hall, shown here when newly opened, replaced it. The building was altered in the 1930s when it lost its 'winter gardens' atmosphere with the removal of much of the glass. The theatre was well known for its summer shows, with many well-known entertainment personalities appearing on its stage. One of the most memorable was in 1959 starring Bruce Forsyth who, between the time of his booking and his appearance, had been named as the compère of the long-running television show *Sunday Night at the London Palladium*.

Above: A view of the interior of the Alexandra Gardens Concert Hall, showing the floral displays for which the Weymouth Council Parks Department were well known.

Left: The floral carpet displayed at the Alexandra Gardens from 31 July to 5 August 1938. This gives further evidence of the parks department's skills.

The illuminations on Weymouth seafront during the summer season and over the Christmas period were a popular feature for many years until replaced by laser lights in 2012. Here Seward's vantage point was from the first floor of a house on the Esplanade.

In 1908 the Pavilion Theatre was constructed, forming a distinctive end to the Esplanade. Touring companies and variety shows performed there and the ballroom was the venue for popular tea dances. Requisitioned by the military authorities in 1939, it reopened in 1950 as the Ritz but its revival was short lived as the auditorium was destroyed in a spectacular fire in April 1954. The foyer and ballroom were relatively undamaged, however, and members of the fire brigade were somewhat disappointed when the site was cleared the following year as they felt that their efforts had largely been wasted!

Those residents of Weymouth who campaigned for many years for skateboarding facilities might be interested in the pictures of the roller-skating facilities provided at the side of the Pavilion on the Pleasure Pier in 1909. This had become a very popular craze and an indoor skating rink at the Jubilee Hall was proving inadequate. The following year the area at the rear of the Pavilion was enclosed to provide an indoor rink. However, roller-skating proved to be a passing attraction and the rink was later converted into the Palm Court Ballroom.

More happy roller skaters enjoying themselves. It is interesting to note the forms of dress for recreation before the advent of designer labels and sportswear!

The *Roebuck* entering the harbour prior to 1914, while holidaymakers take a walk past the roller-skating rink. A steam yacht belonging to one of the more affluent members of the community lies at anchor under the Nothe and the paddle steamer *Albert Victor* is moored alongside the quay.

The cargo stage and ferry steps in the early 1920s. The *Pembroke* is alongside. She was built in 1880 and withdrawn in 1925. A casually stacked pile of barrels blocks the pavement and the ferryman rows a lone passenger across the harbour to the Nothe.

Cosens' paddle steamer *Alexandra* passes the Pavilion while a GWR Channel Islands steamer remains in the harbour. The firm of Cosens had operated from Weymouth since 1845 and its paddle steamers provided day trips to Torquay, Bournemouth, the Isle of Wight, Lulworth Cove and other venues. The use of this vantage point gave Seward a panoramic yet tantalising view, some of the scene being shrouded by trees.

Steam pinnaces transport Royal Naval personnel back to Portland whilst the luggage porter enjoys a smoke after his efforts. Cosens had the contract for ferrying sailors from Weymouth to Portland. The paddle steamer alongside the jetty looks well laden with sailors and a Channel Islands vessel turns in the Cove. All in all, a portrayal of a working harbour.

The gradual transition from sail to steam is well shown in this picture. The sailing vessel *Estafette* of Faversham discharges her cargo and the horses wait patiently whilst the carts are filled. The carts belong to Henry Carter of Weymouth.

The *Antelope* alongside the cargo stage with another vessel astern. Quite what the seafarer is doing peering into the water is a mystery.

At what time of the day did Seward take this photograph? Possibly on a Sunday afternoon? Very few people are in evidence, and the harbour is also similarly deserted. Look at the fine buildings lining Trinity Road, and the old Town Bridge.

The paddle steamer *Empress* departs from Weymouth Harbour with very few passengers on board, whilst the Channel Islands steamer emits large quantities of smoke. Motor launches fill up with passengers for trips round the bay or to see the warships in Portland Harbour. A couple of anglers wait hopefully for a catch. A pleasant day in the early 1920s.

The old Town Bridge facing east from Ferry's Corner, before the motor age! Eight years after the construction of the new bridge in 1930, Ferry's Corner was widened to reduce the sharp curve on the Harbour Tramway.

The old Town Bridge was replaced in 1930. This scene during its demolition includes a train, with contractors' plant much in evidence on the harbour tramway.

This fine warehouse, known to many as the 'Red Warehouse' was built on Custom House Quay in around 1805 and thus predated the present Guildhall, which adjoins the rear of it. The warehouse originally comprised three storeys, a further two being added later. After some years of neglect it was demolished in 1958, a great loss to the local street scene. The advertisement on the adjoining building recalls Strong and Williams, Ironmongers, a firm which occupied a large building at the junction of St Thomas Street and St Edmund Street The crew of motor launch *518* moored alongside have taken the opportunity of a fine day to dry their clothes.

The RMS *St Julien* arriving in the harbour following a journey from the Channel Islands. This vessel, along with her sister ship, *St Helier*, was built in 1925 on the Clyde by John Brown for the Great Western Railway. They served on the Channel Islands route, apart from war service, until 1960 and were remembered with great affection as popular and reliable vessels. Originally built with two funnels, the aft funnels were removed in 1928.

The sender of this card, posted in November 1933, writes 'This photo shows the cranes on the new pier. I am sure you would be interested in watching them moving to and fro as the men unload the cargoes'. The pier and new cargo facilities had been officially opened earlier that year by the Prince of Wales. The vessel shown is *St Patrick* which provided much-needed additional capacity on the Channel Islands service during the summer and which was sunk by bombing whilst on the Fishguard route in 1941.

A congested view of the harbour photographed from the Town Bridge in the 1920s. From left to right can be seen the *Victoria*, the salvage boat *Salvator*, and Cosens' vessels *Premier* and *Emperor of India*. To the extreme left is Templeman's Mills, Helen Lane, a former flour mill which was gutted by fire in 1917.

The RNLI lifeboat *Friern Watch* being launched in 1908. This was the second vessel of this name, the first being given by a Mr Homan in 1887 who donated £2,000 to maintain a lifeboat of that name in perpetuity at Weymouth. The vessel shown in the picture served until 1921. The lifeboat house was extended and rebuilt in 1924.

Gloucester Street Congregational Church was built in 1864 at a cost of £4,465 and was designed by Bennett, a local architect. The twin spires were a prominent feature of Weymouth's skyline. It was a large, imposing building with an interior layout similar to many Nonconformist chapels and a large number of rooms at ground floor level. In 1971 the church was closed following discovery of structural problems and it was demolished in 1980.

Above: Lennox Street, one of the major streets in the Park District, in the 1920s. Adjoining the shop of A.R. Croad, which existed for many years, is Horler's Boot Makers, a type of shop which has all but disappeared. The newspaper billboard refers to an incident in 1928 when a Weymouth Falcon sailing dinghy was damaged by a torpedo that went off course whilst on trials in Weymouth Bay.

Right: The Sailors' Home, later known as the White Ensign Club, St Nicholas Street. This was designed by Crickmay and opened in 1907 and was established following an initiative by the corporation to provide 'accommodation and relaxation of a healthy and homely kind' for sailors. With the gradual decline in the numbers of naval personnel visiting Portland in the 1950s the building was demolished in 1970.

The corner of Maiden Street and St Edmund Street showing the premises of Hurdles, wine merchants and butchers. The attractive cottages in the centre of the picture were demolished in the 1920s to allow an extension to Hurdles' shop.

Park Street in 1911. More specialist shops and conversion to residential property have now replaced the grocers, tobacconist and bakers' shops. In the background is Christ Church, built in 1874. It was affected by declining church attendances and a shortage of clergy by the 1930s, but an offer by a cinema chain to buy the site and re-erect the building in an area that needed a church was rejected. The newly appointed rector closed the church in 1939, stating that it was in poor condition. It served as a British Restaurant during the Second World War and was demolished in 1956. The posters advertise attractions such as excursions to Killarney and London, and Milledge's auction at Portland.

The opposite side of Park Street four years earlier with a group of youngsters posing for, or perhaps teasing, the cameraman. The large building at the end of the street is the Queens Hotel.

Seward often photographed the everyday scene. What connection the sender had in 1907 with Wesley Street is not recorded. The postcard was sent to a lady in Bruton informing her that the sender would come home on the 5.17 p.m. train, with an invitation to visit later that evening. Whilst life has changed, in that the sender today would no doubt send a message, or text, by mobile phone, Wesley Street has not changed greatly in appearance except for the fact that it has been pedestrianised.

Ranelagh Road prior to 1914. This street has been the subject of a pleasing enhancement in recent years, with echelon-style parking on the west side.

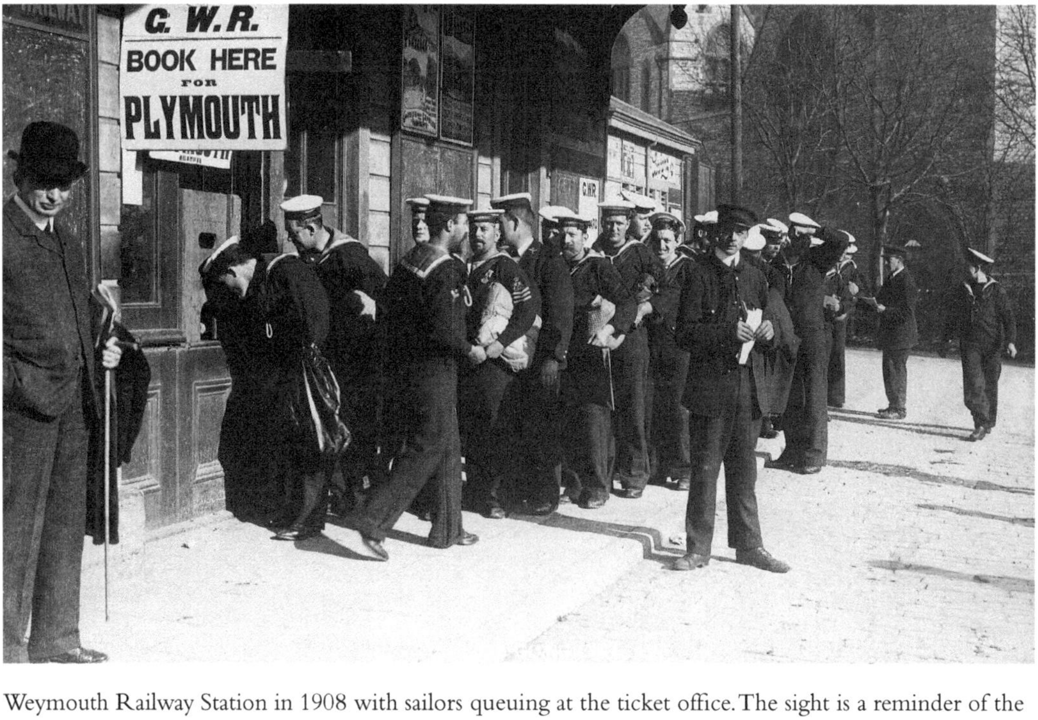

Weymouth Railway Station in 1908 with sailors queuing at the ticket office. The sight is a reminder of the heavy use of the line by naval personnel between the two ports. By that date the railway station was fifty years old and consideration was being given to its replacement from around 1913. A new platform was built in 1957 and this forms the basis of the present station, opened in 1986.

Brownlow Street prior to 1914, looking towards St John's Church. Two horse-drawn milk floats containing milk churns are the only sign of life, and even then only one has the horse with it. The milliner's shop advertises itself as an agent for Thomson's Dye Works in Perth – possibly to allow ladies to dye their summer hats. The lack of congestion is a change from the present day scene.

Turton Street may seem an unusual choice for a postcard, but photographer Seward lived in No. 13 when this picture was taken during the winter of 1913.

Many Weymouthians whose memories go back to the 1950s will remember the Rose Walk in Melcombe Regis Gardens. These gardens were laid out in the 1920s following a land reclamation scheme and included a bowling green, tennis courts, gardens and the council nurseries. Gradually from the mid-1960s the gardens were converted to car parking and all that remains of the original layout is the bowling green.

A lady looks doubtfully at swans in 1910 – was she in danger of getting wet feet or being attacked by an angry swan? The picture was taken before the construction of Westham Embankment Bridge in 1921 and the subsequent reclamation. On the left of the picture is Commercial Road.

Boats for hire alongside Commercial Road on a murky day before 1909. Before the formation of Radipole Lake by the construction of Westham Bridge in 1921 it was possible to row (or be rowed) up the River Wey to Radipole. Also prominent is the original railway bridge on the Portland line, replaced in 1909.

Alexandra Terrace, Commercial Road, was built in 1864 and marked the western boundary of Melcombe Regis before the major land reclamations of the 1920s. The Portland Railway Hotel is now no longer in use as a public house. The houses to the right of the picture were subsequently demolished to provide the Commercial Road frontage for Weymouth Bus station.

A pleasant interlude rowing on Radipole Lake. A swan passes rather close for comfort to the oar – both for the rower and the swan! A train waits at Melcombe Regis Station.

This card, which was posted in September 1913, shows the swans with Melcombe Regis Station in the background. The writer of the card comments to the recipient in London 'Just lovely weather. We are just going for a sea trip'. That sums up an ideal holiday at a seaside resort in those far-off days.

The swan herd followed by youthful volunteer apprentices comes to feed the swans at the side of Radipole Park Drive in the 1930s. On the far left of the picture (underneath the bridge) can be seen the stern of the dredger which periodically kept the reeds down in Radipole Lake. A local competition was run to give it a suitable name – one suggestion was the 'Dredgenought'! The condition of this vessel deteriorated and it was eventually scrapped.

The statue of Queen Victoria, Greenhill, photographed in 1905. The bronze statue was unveiled in 1902 to commemorate her long reign. The railings were removed many years ago and the monument is now on an island on heavily-trafficked Greenhill. In 1958 the statue achieved widespread press coverage when it was daubed with paint by University Students on a trip from London, which led to their subsequent appearance in the local Magistrates' Court.

Greenhill Gardens were laid out in the 1870s on land belonging to Sir Frederick Johnstone, who owned much of the land in the Dorchester Road and Greenhill area. The view shows gravelled walks and tall hedges, but the gardens have been extended and developed during the twentieth century and now include tennis courts, a bowling green and a putting course.

The Floral Clock in Greenhill Gardens was a popular feature for many years but the hands became the target for vandalism and the display was discontinued in the 1960s.

A popular place to pause for refreshment was the Greenhill Gardens Café. The writer of the card, who sent it to his aunt in Dorchester states that he 'arrived in good time and got fixed up at once'. The tariff indicates that the inclusive charge for afternoon tea was one shilling and two pence.

A popular facility at the northern end of the Esplanade is the terrace of beach chalets at Greenhill, which was constructed in the 1920s. These were enjoyed by the local residents and continue to be so today.

The Putting Green, Greenhill Gardens, happily still in existence. Greenhill Gardens were extended in the 1920s to include a bowling green, tennis courts, putting green and beach chalets all within easy reach of the beach.

This tree-lined peaceful view of Dorchester Road looking towards Lodmoor Hill before the First World War is in sharp contrast to the bustling traffic-filled present day scene.

A Great Western Railway bus passes Lodmoor Hill in the direction of Radipole Spa around 1925. Whilst the view is recognisable today, the number of trees has diminished but the traffic has not!

Avenue Road in around 1912 showing the tree-lined pavements, a feature of many side roads in the borough.

Glendinning Avenue, another such road. This street was developed from the 1890s and consisted of large houses, some of which employed uniformed maids until the 1930s.

The Nothe Walk was a popular destination for a stroll where one could view the shipping in the harbour, go fishing on the stone pier or climb up to the Nothe to obtain a good view of the Royal Navy ships in Portland Harbour. This photograph was taken in 1924.

The Girls' Friendly Society Hostel, North Quay. This was operated in connection with Holy Trinity Church and was later renamed Sowter Lodge in memory of a former vicar. The building was demolished along with most of the buildings in North Quay in the summer of 1961. The Council Offices which were built on the site and opened in 1971 were themselves closed in 2016 and await an uncertain future.

High Street, Weymouth, in the years before the First World War. This picturesque street described in 1774 as 'very narrow and irregular' had been the bustling medieval High Street of the old town of Weymouth. By the Second World War it was in decline and the bombing of Chapelhay in 1940 accelerated this. The only buildings in the photograph still in existence are the Coffee Tavern on the extreme right (now Kingdom Hall), which was built in 1875 as a temperance pub, and Holy Trinity Church.

High West Street, Weymouth, in about 1910. On the left there were a number of streets with small tightly packed houses, which were demolished in the mid-1930s to form part of the site for the fire station. The buildings on the right are largely recognisable today. The barber's shop later became a grocer's and was accessed from Boot Hill.

The Old Town Hall, High Street. Apart from the lack of railings and the replacement of the building on the extreme right (as a result of war damage) the scene looks remarkably similar today. The posters advertise a variety of attractions including Professor Lorenzo's Wonderful Dogs, a trip to Ascot Races and the customary auction notices.

An atmospheric view looking west from North Quay. A train to Portland labours up the bank to Rodwell Station and in the Backwater a small number of boats contrast with today's busy scene. Westwey Road has not yet been built, nor have the major extensions to the gasworks of 1932.

The Sidney Hall, at the corner of Newstead Road and Boot Hill, was opened in 1900 and cost £8,000. It was given to the Parish of Holy Trinity by Sir John Groves, the brewer, in memory of his son, Sidney, who had died in 1895. It was intended for use by the Church Lads' Brigade in which Sidney had served as an officer. With the demise of that organisation the main hall was used for a variety of purposes, and the small hall at the rear was used largely for church activities. Following wartime damage to Holy Trinity School in Chapelhay the Sidney Hall was used as temporary accommodation for its pupils. The 1950s saw the main hall leased out for roller skating. It was demolished in 1987 when the Asda supermarket was built.

A Great Western Railway Milnes-Daimler bus pauses on Boot Hill to allow passengers to alight, whilst a reminder of a more traditional form of transport can be seen on the opposite side of the road. On the left can be seen the Edwards Homes, ten cottages built in 1894 as a gift by Sir Henry Edwards who served as MP for Weymouth from 1867 to 1885. He was a great benefactor to the town, providing these and Edwardsville, Rodwell Avenue, for the aged poor of Weymouth. Among his other benefactions were an annual dinner for residents aged over seventy, the Working Men's Club in Mitchell Street, and the mechanism of the Jubilee Clock.

The Nothe headland had been a traditional open space for the benefit of the local populace but the building of the Nothe Fort in the 1860s led to controversy and lengthy negotiations to resolve the question of public access. It took until 1888 to lay out the gardens, which were extended in 1909. This card was sent two years later. The Nothe area has suffered from erosion over the years. In 1960 the council bought the Fort and much of the surrounding military property from the Ministry of Defence and now the Fort is leased to Weymouth Civic Society as a popular tourist attraction.

Another view of the Nothe Gardens with its layout of walks. In the background Royal Naval vessels are anchored in the bay.

Newton's Cove looking towards the Nothe in the 1920s. A great expansion of Great Western shipping traffic had taken place by the late 1880s. The company had looked for alternative accommodation and decided to build a new harbour with connecting railway at Newton's Cove. Despite opposition from the council which stood to lose revenue, the appropriate legislation was passed in 1898. The scheme was abandoned in 1913, but not before a public house, optimistically named the Railway Dock Hotel, had been built in 1902.

The description of this postcard, posted in 1911 is 'Portland train from Sandsfoot Castle'. The Portland line ran from Weymouth along the Chesil bank to Victoria Square and then climbed along the cliffs to its terminus at Easton, the later part of the journey being very spectacular. Sadly the line was closed to passengers in 1952 and to freight in 1965. The photograph is taken from the site of Castle Cove Sailing Club. Much erosion has taken place here since and the line of the footpath has been obliterated.

'Bincleaves Chine' is the photographer's rather picturesque name for Castle Cove. The photograph, taken in 1911, shows the beach and Underbarn Walk leading to Bincleaves and the Nothe. Large houses in Belle Vue Road are beginning to be built and prominent in the photograph is Glenthorne, Old Castle Road.

Sandsfoot Castle had been built in the reign of Henry VIII but its site suffered from erosion by the sea. The land in front of the castle is seen here in the 1920s laid out as tennis courts prior to its acquisition by the council in 1929. Three years later the area was laid out as the 'Tudor Gardens'. This was a good vantage point to view the many shipping movements in Portland Harbour.

An imposing view of Sandsfoot Castle in 1926 photographed from the seashore.

St Paul's Church, Westham, was consecrated in 1900 and completed in 1913. This photograph, which was taken in 1935, shows not an advertisement for church activities but a cinema poster for the film *Captain Blood* starring Errol Flynn. The bungalow to the right of the picture was demolished and is now the site of St Paul's Vicarage.

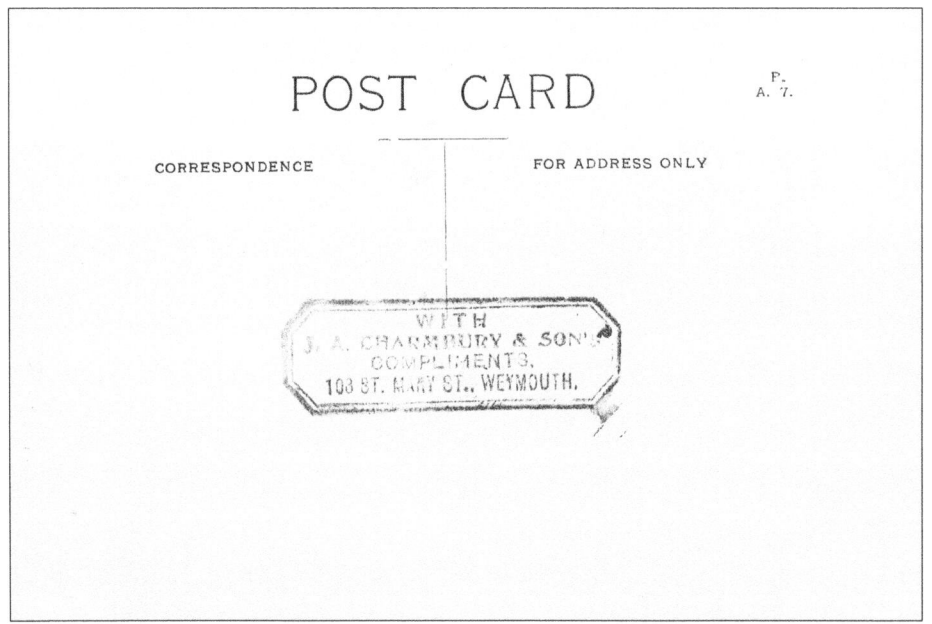

A stamp from J.A. Charmbury & Sons. He operated from No. 103 St Mary's Street as a tobacconist and also specialised in supplying goods to naval and military messes and canteens. He also sold Edwin Seward's postcards. Mr Charmbury was a prominent local councillor.

two

Around Portland

Crowds swarm ashore from Cosens' paddle steamer *Premier* at Castletown before 1914. Stone awaits shipment from wagons on the pier. Although built in 1846, the *Premier* had nearly thirty more years of life, not being withdrawn until 1938. This trip has been revived in recent years with motor vessel excursions from Weymouth to Portland Castle. This was a popular destination, seven trips being made daily by the paddlers.

Cosens' paddle steamer *Victoria* landing passengers at Church Ope Cove in 1911. This trip took place occasionally in connection with charitable fundraising events. The passengers took tea at Pennsylvania Castle. At least one of these cruises helped to raise funds for the new All Saints Church, Portland.

Portland Roads with, to the right, HMS *Boscawen*, which served as a training ship at Portland from 1866 to 1905. This was the second ship called *Boscawen*, she took the name after her arrival in 1874.

The Fleet in Portland Roads – a card posted in 1911. This shows a large number of vessels including the *Agamemnon, Lord Nelson* and *Collingwood*. In the years before the widespread use of telephones, postcards were a popular method of communication. The picture at times seemed irrelevant to the sender as in this case where the writer 'Maud' is lamenting the loss of her brooch!

A light vessel was first stationed at the Shambles in 1859 and a succession of vessels followed it, until the last vessel was replaced by two buoys in 1976. The light was extinguished in 1940 and the vessel laid up in Portland Harbour for the duration of the Second World War. The Shambles Lightship in the picture served from 1883 to 1947.

A floating dock at Portland, which served the Dockyard. It arrived in 1914, went away for the First World War, then returned until 1940. It allowed vessels to be repaired without the delay of sending them to other dockyards which had better docking facilities.

Castletown had prospered as a result of the Royal Navy and by the date of this postcard, 1905, resembled the hinterlands of many Naval establishments with outfitters and other associated businesses and architecturally impressive public houses.

Twenty-five years later a sailor crosses the road in front of the ornate Royal Breakwater Hotel while some of his shipmates stroll up towards the Portland Roads public house.

The Salvation Army Sailors' Home and Score's Steam Bakery and Naval Contractors and Ships Chandlers, at Castletown in the 1920s. The writer of the card comments 'the rails are not tram lines – can't afford them down here but a four wheeled vehicle which carries slabs of rock upon it now uses it.'

Castletown in 1906 taken outside the post office. The writer of the card, sent to his friend in Southsea, gives news that the fleet arrived that day so there was plenty of work to do. He also comments that 'Tom and his chum' are to be seen at the first floor window.

Portland Castle in 1910. This was originally built in 1539 to shelter shipping in Portland Roads and contains some fine examples of masons' craftsmanship. It is now under the control of English Heritage and is a popular tourist and historical attraction.

A traction engine, its trailers loaded with stone, passes Victoria Gardens on the way to F.J. Barnes' sawmills in Victoria Square in 1924. The writer of the card comments 'this is where you land on the bus from Weymouth'. The vehicle was later owned by Richard Townsend's Amusements of Chickerell and rebuilt by Eddisons of Dorchester as a showman's engine 'Queen Mary', and is now in preservation.

Fishermen at Chesil in 1907. The box bears the name 'Pitman – Weymouth' recalling a well-known family of fish wholesalers in the town.

A thatched cottage in Little Brandy Row, the thatch reeds possibly having come from Radipole Lake. Behind is a small courtyard giving access to a number of other small properties. Whilst the building was partially demolished in 1905, the doorway remains in the wall of a fisherman's store.

Whether this photograph was posed is unclear but one can hope that the people sitting on the edge of the rowing boat took expert advice before setting off, in view of the currents in the area. Once again one can only marvel at what we would consider the unsuitability of clothing for such an activity.

The junction of High Street with Chiswell, probably in the 1920s. The shop on the left of the picture has a rack of postcards for sale. Could they be some of Edwin Seward's? Chiswell Post Office acts as an agent for dye works. On the opposite side of the road is a bakers. Perhaps they sold the local delicacy of Portland – dough cakes. Cleall's the grocer is at the end of the row and like many grocers of that era has a sign advertising Fry's chocolate.

The woman pushing the pram in the 1920s would not be safe if she attempted that journey along Chiswell today. In the middle of the road is a large stone cistern, which stored water for domestic use.

Fortuneswell was the main shopping area for Underhill, although this is not evident from the lack of residents in the photograph. D. Lawrence, the butcher, is proud of his appointment as a Government Contractor. On the opposite side of the road is a leather goods merchant, a trade seldom seen today.

Children pose for the camera outside St John's Church in Fortuneswell before the First World War. Meanwhile hawkers ply their trade. One of the girls on the pavement has a basket perhaps ready to do the shopping.

This is a photograph of the bottom of Mallams, Portland. It shows the Royal Oak Inn, a public house owned by John Groves. Portland had a high proportion of public houses, probably because of its naval and military connections.

The top of the Merchants Incline with loaded wagons about to start their descent to Castletown for shipment. This railway carried stone from the quarries at the top of the island to the loading pier at Castletown.

The lower end of the Merchants Incline in around 1910, with two horses hauling the loaded stone wagons away to Castletown. Some empty wagons wait to ascend the incline.

The 'Captain's House' – a small eighteenth-century mansion built for a wealthy stone merchant. It was never actually built for a captain. After many years of dereliction it was restored in the 1990s.

The Verne Citadel was built in the 1860s and was used for military purposes until 1945. Here the 1st Battalion the Somerset Regiment march out from the South Gate between 1908 and 1911. In 1949 it was taken over as a prison and new buildings were erected inside the Citadel.

Easton Lane near its junction with Grove Road around 1910. The Portland Steam Laundry's horse has a refreshment break at the fountain. The whole scene is a tremendous contrast to that of today.

Easton, looking towards the site of the previous view. Many of the buildings are recognisable today, if not the businesses occupying them.

The laying of the foundation stone of All Saints Church, Portland, in May 1914 by the Bishop of Salisbury. This was built nearer the centre of the parish as a replacement for St George's Church. All Saints, designed by the local architect Crickmay, contains fine carved choir stalls. It is unusual that the foundation stone was laid and the building completed during the First World War.

The interior of All Saints Church, Portland. On the chancel roof can be seen unusual panels depicting the signs of the zodiac.

Easton Gardens, showing the Clock Tower and bandstand. Easton Gardens, laid out in 1904, provided a focal point for Easton. The bandstand, upon which band concerts were given for sixty years, was removed in 1965 due to lack of maintenance.

The Children's Parade at Church Ope Cove, Wednesday 5 August 1931. This cove can be reached by 125 steps and whilst the fishermen's huts are now used for recreational purposes, the cove has been used for transport of stone, fishing, and smuggling.

Weston looking north, showing the pond in around 1904.

St Andrew's Church, also known as 'Avalanche Church' was designed by Crickmay and opened in 1879 as a memorial to those drowned in the collision between two vessels, the *Avalanche* and *Forest,* off Portland two years previously. In this maritime disaster many lives were lost.

Landslips affecting the railway line to Easton were not uncommon, as shown in this view taken in 1907. Much of this section of line was of unstable Kimmeridge clay and automatic signals operated by trip wires were installed in an attempt to avert accidents.

Rufus Castle, known locally as Bow and Arrow Castle, is a pre-fifteenth-century fortress built to defend Church Ope Cove from attacks by invaders from the sea.

Right: Seward photographed the famous Pulpit Rock, a view which has been replicated many times since. One can only wonder who posed for the photographer.

Below: William Moore and his son were contracted to build a new highway between Priory Quarries and Underhill in 1810. This view, taken from above Tillycoombe in the 1920s, shows New Road and Old Hill. Whilst Old Hill was no longer used for vehicular traffic, in the 1960s the then Clerk of the Urban District Council exercised the legal right to drive his car up this ancient highway.

A traction engine hauls a wagon loaded with stone down New Road, apparently on the wrong side of the road to enable it to take the corner safely at the junction of New Road and Fortuneswell. This is still a hazard today and large stone lorries have been known to get stuck. The Travellers Rest public house was converted to residential accommodation in the 1960s.

Unveiling of the War Memorial at Yeates, Portland, on 11 November 1926. The memorial contains the names of 223 Portlanders killed during the First World War and was unveiled by former Private Crispin, three of whose brothers had been casualties. It is one of the finest locations for such a memorial, overlooking West Bay. Each year a memorial service is held here on Remembrance Sunday.

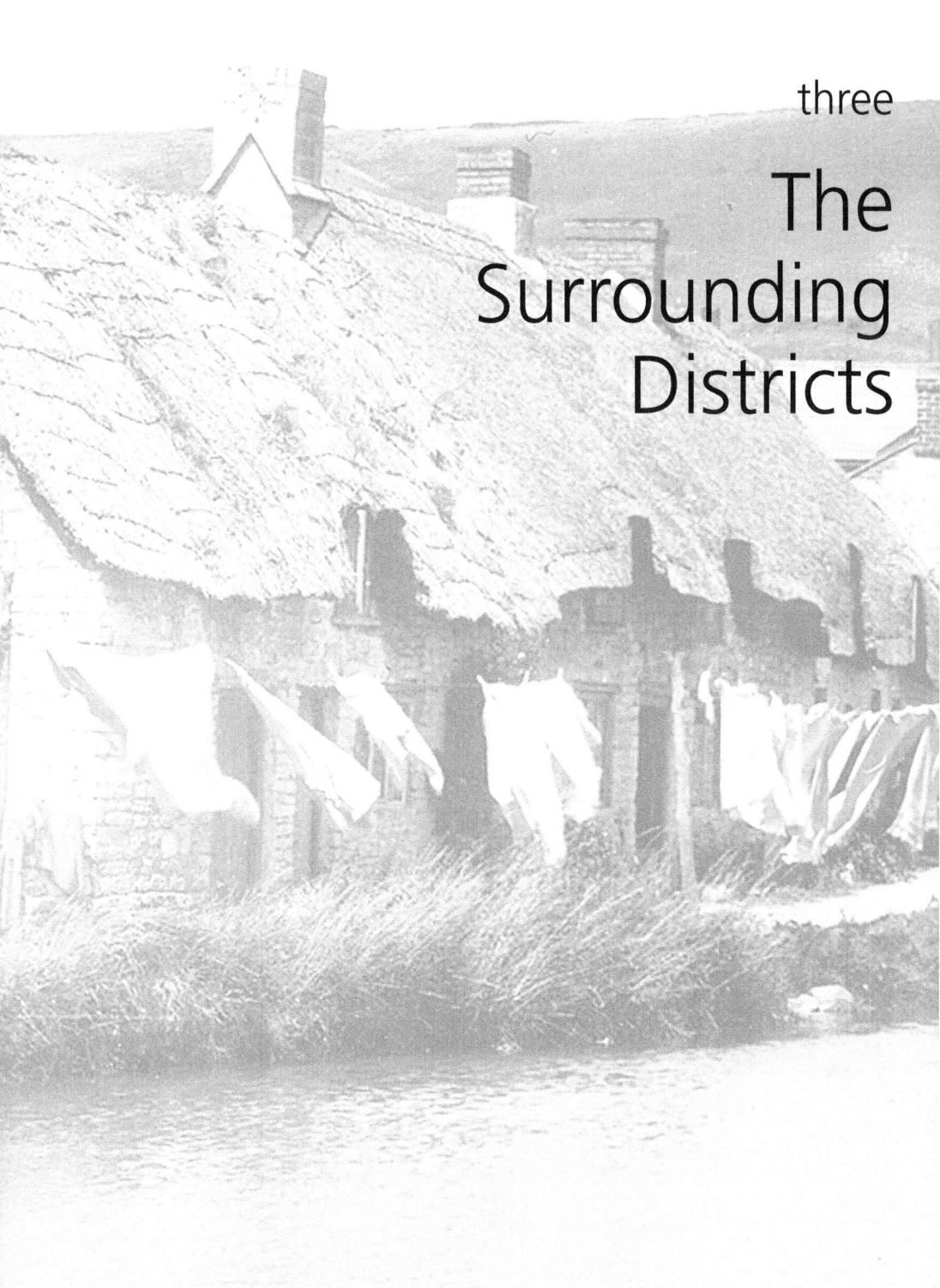

three

The Surrounding Districts

Spa Road, Radipole, in the snow, around 1910. The corrugated iron Congregational Church was opened in 1905 and rebuilt in the 1950s. Apart from that, the view today is largely unchanged but sadly the successor to Brine's Grocers and Confectioners closed in 2004 when it ceased to be a post office.

Radipole Lane at its junction with Spa Road prior to the First World War, looking towards the rectory. The tidal area behind the cyclists has since silted up. Since 1921, when the sluices at Westham Bridge were installed, the area has become a meadow. Boat trips up the River Wey to Radipole were a popular attraction for residents and visitors in the early years of the twentieth century.

A view from Southill looking over Radipole Village. Prominent in the photograph is the thirteenth-century St Ann's Church, the mother church of Melcombe Regis, with Radipole Old Manor to its right. The Victorian Radipole Manor to the left is set in large grounds with a lodge at each of its two entrances.

A closer look at the Old Manor which was built in the sixteenth century. In the early years of the twentieth century it was in poor condition but was carefully restored under the ownership of Captain and Mrs Legh just before the Second World War.

Nottington showing one of many rural walks. One of the most notable aspects of Nottington is the Spa, the waters of which were described in *Commin's Directory* of 1829 as 'tasting like a very hard boiled egg'!

Present day motorists queuing on Dorchester Road at the junction with Littlemoor Road may have noticed this building on the west side of Dorchester Road. It was restored in the 1960s. One of the other contrasts is the almost complete absence of any form of vehicular traffic and people.

Dorchester Road, Upwey, looking towards the Royal Standard public house. The cart bears the inscription '1 and 2 The Market'.

The Royal Oak, Upwey, in the 1920s. This was demolished in the late 1960s for road improvements. The steep Roman road leads straight to Dorchester and a new road with a hairpin bend was constructed in 1824. This was in turn replaced with the Weymouth Relief Road which opened in 2011.

Upwey Wishing Well was a popular venue for a visit in the 1920s particularly by 'Sugar'em Shorey's' horse bus which ran from the King's Statue.

A view of St Laurence Church, Upwey, in 1924. This church dates from the fifteenth century but was heavily restored from Victorian times. The road to the Winterbornes climbs Gould's Hill behind the church.

It would be difficult to recognise this rural scene of Littlemoor in the 1930s when compared with today's largely developed suburb.

A Great Western Railway Maudslay bus heads from Preston towards Weymouth in 1922. Preston was then a small village outside the borough and in 1931, two years before the borough boundaries were extended to include the village, the population was only 855. The developments off Coombe Valley Road and at Southdown started in the late 1950s.

This view of Preston Road in 1933 looks towards the Ship Inn and the junction with Sutton Road. Considerable road widening has taken place since. The sender of this card comments 'where Dawn took Jimmy junior and myself for our first evening drive. She drove very well indeed, and, of course the moonlight helped'.

The Mill Pond at Sutton Poyntz with little to disturb this idyllic view. The chimney is part of Sutton Poyntz water pumping station and dates from 1897. By the 1950s some of the cottages were in poor condition but were rebuilt in a sympathetic style.

Perhaps this was taken on a Monday – washing day at Sutton Poyntz!

The White Horse at Osmington was carved in 1808 and measures 280ft long and 323ft high. It was carved to commemorate the visit of George III three years after his last visit. He never actually saw the carving but it is so famous that it would be an obvious subject for Seward.

Poxwell, with a cyclist about to ride off whilst a resident is deep in conversation with a courier. Few would recognise this as the now busy road out of Weymouth.

Bowleaze Cove in 1929. Soon after, the area started to develop as an attractive alternative to the main beach, and campsites and, later, caravan parks were developed. The art deco Riviera Hotel was built in 1937 and the present panorama bears little similarity to the somewhat rustic scene portrayed here.

Waddon Manor, east of Portesham, was built in 1651 but later reduced in size. It is on a pleasant by-road from Portesham and perhaps Seward enjoyed watching the lambing in spring from this vantage point.

A pleasant view looking east towards All Saints Church, Wyke Regis. The old village is a conservation area and much of its charm has been retained.

Wyke High Street in around 1910 looking north, with Castle Hill Road on the left. The second property on the left is the former Masons Arms public house and the thatched cottages in the middle of the picture were burnt down in 1926. Did Edwin Seward get the children in the picture to pose or did they arrive there by chance?

Wyke Square photographed after 1905, the date of the erection of the first gas lamp in the square. In the centre is the Albert Inn. Adjoining the Swan Inn can be seen the entrance to Hamilton House, one time property of James Hamilton who designed many of the public buildings in Weymouth including St Mary's Church. Next to this is the entrance to the slaughterhouse.

Dr Andrew Fenoulhet built Wyke Castle at the top of Pirates Lane in about 1855. It has been suggested that the property was designed to face south in the direction of his beloved native country – France – but other research suggests that he came from London.

An important centre of maritime safety was the coastguard station at Wyke Regis. A Coastguard Officer's house (now Centre House) was built around 1845 and in 1886 further houses were added. The operations centre moved to Portland in 1976, and in 1988 to the Old Customs House in Custom House Quay, but the Wyke Regis Auxiliary Coastguard team still use the premises. Many coastguards were ex-naval personnel.

The Torpedo Works in Wyke Regis were founded in 1891 to produce torpedoes for the Admiralty, who were only prepared to buy them if they were made in Britain. By 1907 it was called the Whitehead Torpedo Works (Weymouth) and produced torpedoes for the next fourteen years until going into liquidation in 1921. In 1923 the factory reopened and produced armaments for the next forty years.

Buxton Road after 1905, looking east from Foord's Corner with 'Stormount' the only house visible. The sender of this card comments, 'This is the road I travelled to the camp from Weymouth. It was coming up the hill that I was stopped by the military police and ordered to button my coat. PS take care of these cards it is all the views that I can get here'.

Seward took this picture of Market Street in Abbotsbury. The shopkeeper hangs up the blinds while children pose in the almost deserted street. The scene contrasts with that of today, when at the time of writing residents have again expressed serious concern at the increasing number of heavy vehicles attempting to negotiate its narrow corners.

Another view of Abbotsbury showing two of the swans for which the village is famous.

The Cattistock Hunt outside the Ilchester Arms at Abbotsbury. In the background is Abbotsbury School and cottages that belong to the Strangways estate. A large number of people have turned out to watch the hounds.

Seward did not confine his photography solely to Weymouth and Portland. This postcard is of Fleet Lane, Chickerell, a settlement three miles from Weymouth. Whilst posted in 1936 the picture recalls an earlier age with the cows being moved down the lane whilst the cowman with his stick poses for the photographer.

four

Events

A fire at Park Mead, Wyke Regis, on Saturday 12 January 1907 attracted a great deal of public interest and led to the loss of three thatched cottages. Following the alarm being raised at about 8.00 p.m. coastguards, sailors, tradesmen and workers from Whitehead Torpedo Works rushed to help and at about 8.20 p.m. the fire brigade was telephoned. News soon spread and a large number of people rushed to the fire station at St Edmund Street to watch the brigade turn out. The steam fire engine could not leave the fire station in St Edmund Street, as there was a delay in bringing the horses which were stabled a mile away in Holly Road. By 9.00 p.m. there was no sign of the horses so a wagon was commandeered and six firemen were sent on to Wyke with a quantity of hose. There were jeers from the crowd and the *Southern Times*, catering for erudite readership, reported that the firemen who remained 'were indignant as the people themselves and inwardly anathematised the antiquated arrangements'. Shortly afterwards the horses arrived and the engine moved off, followed by hundreds of residents who went by foot, motor and bike, and buses were full to overflowing. The *Southern Times* commented that whilst there, the firemen 'worked like Trojans but their work was hampered by the many thousands of spectators, some of whom with complete indifference trampled on the hose'. The paper reported 'on Sunday a great many people visited the scene of the fire, picture postcards of which are selling rapidly in Weymouth'. This postcard can be presumed to be one of these!

The wedding of the year in Weymouth took place on Tuesday 11 June 1907. Hilda Templeman, daughter of Alderman Thomas John Templeman, married Stanley Readhead of Westoe, South Shields, at St John's Church. The bridegroom was a shipbuilder. The Templemans lived at Stanton Court on the Esplanade and this photograph shows the wedding guests leaving the church and going towards Stanton Court. Hilda had served as her father's mayoress in 1897/8 and also for the two and half years prior to her wedding. The wedding merited four columns in the *Southern Times*, giving accounts of the service, the dresses of the bride and her six bridesmaids, the flowers, the guests and the presents. Among the presents were a silver light-fluted ornament with three massive branches and bowls from the town council, a gold bracelet inlaid with turquoise and pearl from the borough officers, a silver salver from the justices, a solid silver chatelaine purse from the corporation employees and a Crown Staffordshire coffee set from the Conservative party. Although the weather during the day itself was fine, it rained heavily in the evening which meant that the Alexandra Gardens could not be illuminated in honour of the event as had been arranged. The rain however did not postpone the concert where Chevalier Bocchi conducted the band playing a piece called 'Cortege Nuptiale' which he had written especially for the wedding. Seward's postcard shows the fashions of the time well, especially the hats that were commented upon in the papers as being full of ruches of roses and feathers! It is noteworthy that the postcard was posted on 14 June, showing how topical Seward's postcards were.

There must have been a large market for Seward's cards of particular events. This shows the opening of the Sailors' Home in St Nicholas Street by Lord Tweedmouth, First Lord of the Admiralty. The writer of this card, posted in July 1907, makes scant mention of the event but comments to the recipient in Broadwey 'I should have been out to see you but have paper-hangers and painters in. Goodness knows when they will finish. What miserable weather'.

St Paul's Church annual fête took place on Wednesday 24 June 1908 in a field adjoining Westdowne, Chickerell Road. The event had many attractions including a grand masquerade procession, open-air concerts, novel and interesting sideshows, and shooting gallery. The procession includes a cow and a lamb, both of which appear unconcerned by the activities going on round them. The *Southern Times* reported that the sun shone and 'in the dancing ring a gay crowd of Terpsichoreans tripped it lightly over the greensward and made merry with the last hours which remained of a memorable and pleasant day'!

In November 1908 Frederick Sefton Smith became Mayor and on the Sunday after the annual meeting of the council the mayor and corporation processed from the Guildhall to St Mary's Church for the Civic Service. This was traditionally one of the highlights of the Civic Year. He would be attended by the borough justices, borough police and the fire brigade and on occasions service detachments. The street scene is fairly easily recognisable but the Market House on the far side of St Mary's Church was demolished in 1939.

The band waiting to escort the Mayor from St Mary's Church in November 1908.

Empire Day on 24 May had been normally observed each year since 1904. In the years immediately before 1909 the day became more widely celebrated. Prior to that year celebrations had taken place at individual schools when children saluted the flag and sang the National Anthem. In 1909, however, the mayor, Frederick Sefton Smith, spoke in favour of the observance taking place at the King's Statue. The *Southern Times* reported that the Borough Education Committee expressed concern at this suggestion, stating that the 'risk of bringing 2,000 children from their respective schools to the heart of the town would be too severe a strain to be imposed on teachers'. However objections were overcome and the scheme proposed by the mayor was carried out. The postcard shows the ceremony underway with the children all lined up with the teachers at the end of the rows. At 9.30 a.m. the blowing of a cornet gave the sign for the Union Jack to be unfurled and this was saluted by the children. Kipling's 'Recessional' was then sung to add to the sound of guns fired from the battleships in the harbour. The schools originally taking part were St Mary's, St John's, St Augustine's, Holy Trinity and Cromwell Road, but St Augustine's withdrew at the last minute and held a separate event at Queen Victoria's Statue. The newspapers of the day commented upon the 'orderliness which prevailed throughout' and gave great praise to the teachers for training their pupils. They also wrote that the eyes of the children 'shone with patriotism'. Each child was given a souvenir and an orange. The fact it was a hot day is clear from the parasols which are evident in the photograph.

Immediately following this ceremony the Mayor, Corporation and Borough officials assembled at Ferry Steps for the ceremony of Beating of the Bounds which was being revived after a gap of thirteen years. This involved a fifteen-mile walk around the borough where individuals (children and adults) were 'bumped' at each boundary stone. One of the officers attending was the newly-appointed Sanitary Inspector Frank Fanner who had been one of the boys bumped thirteen years previously and had brought with him the half crown which he had been given on that occasion. In common with many such events, the Beating of the Bounds was not without its unscripted moments. These started when one of the civic party, Cllr Charmbury, was rowed across the harbour 'unaware that his coat tails were swishing gently through the water'. The procession made its way to each of the boundary stones where members of the council were 'bumped'. This postcard shows a boy being bumped at one of the stones. Obviously from their faces it was an event that was enjoyed by many. At Sandesfort Hill the edict was given that councillors were to be bumped. The *Weymouth Telegram* reported that 'getting to work in earnest the Mayor removed his coat and enlisted the help of the Town Clerk. These two gentlemen with memories of protracted council meetings treated the worthy but talkative councillors in none too gentle a manner'. Unfortunately at Markham House, Wyke Road, the Mayor had to scale a wall and a Mr Gale sprained his leg. At the junction of Chickerell and Abbotsbury Roads twelve boys were bumped and at the seventh stone the son of the Town Clerk and a press representative were similarly treated. Edwin Seward was not the official photographer but followed the party around and this is one of the photographs he took.

In 1908 the Mayor and Corporation process to St Paul's Church in state, headed by a contingent of the Borough Police Force. Weymouth and Melcombe Regis had its own force until it was merged with the Dorset Constabulary in 1921.

The arrival of a circus was a great spectacle, especially for children. The circus train would arrive at the railway station and when unloaded the animals would process (in cages where necessary) to the ground. Here a number of children at the foot of Trinity Steps eagerly await its arrival.

The funeral of Seargant Major Frederick James Jacobs of the 28th Company RGA who died on 14 June 1908 aged thirty-seven. The funeral procession left the Red Barracks, the coffin being transported on a gun carriage via Hope Square, St Thomas Street and Abbotsbury Road to Holy Trinity cemetery. The band of the 2nd Liverpool Regiment from Bovington Camp took part. The route was lined with sympathisers and the cortege took one hour to reach the cemetery.

At the interment of Seargant Major Jacobs a volley was fired over the grave and the Last Post played.

Angus Valdimar Hambro MP addresses the crowds from the Hotel Burdon following his election victory as the Conservative candidate in January 1910. He had defeated the sitting Liberal member. There was an 89.1 percent turnout to vote! He served as constituency member for Dorset Southern from 1910 until 1922 and then as MP for Dorset North from 1937 to 1945. He was also a member of Dorset County Council. Early in his career as an MP he announced his intention to divide his parliamentary salary between the hospitals of Dorchester and Weymouth and other charitable causes.

The death of King Edward VII on Friday 6 May 1910 was marked with a special council meeting, and the local newspaper *Southern Times* was black edged in accordance with tradition. Guns were fired in tribute at the Nothe, as shown in this photograph.

The Royal Southern Counties Show on Tuesday 13 June was held on a thirty-acre site off Dorchester Road. It was judged to be a success, attracting 1,121 entries and a record number of sheep. Special trains were provided to transport visitors. Distinguished guests included Lord Digby, the MP and the Mayor of Dorchester. Here, the Mayor (Cllr R.C. Watts) and other dignitaries line up for the official opening.

Coronation Day, Thursday 22 June 1911, was celebrated in a wide variety of ways. Church services were held and a great crowd assembled at the King's Statue for a civic service. By this time heavy rain had set in and many of the programmed events including the school sports had to be delayed until the following day – a weather pattern repeated in coronation year in 1953.

Left: Later that afternoon the Mayor, Cllr R.C. Watts, planted a coronation tree in the Alexandra Gardens, supported by the Town Clerk and the Chaplain, the Revd T.L. Lancaster, Rector of St Mary's (both of whom managed to shelter from the rain). Richard Caines Watts was a director of John Groves the local brewery and played a prominent part in the public life of the borough. For ten years he served as chairman of the local hospital committee and a ward was named in his memory at Weymouth and District Hospital.

Below: King George V visited Weymouth on Saturday 11 May 1912 whilst inspecting the fleet. The Fleet Review had been delayed due to the Royal Yacht being fog bound at Yarmouth. In this photograph the King is meeting the Mayor, R.C. Watts, with numerous civic dignitaries lined up. The borough fire brigade were also in attendance!

Crowds lined the Esplanade by Ferry Steps to see the King depart from the Pier in Weymouth. A policeman and sailors stand to attention; other members of the crowd raise their hats in respect. The town had put up flags to welcome the King.

Admiral Lord Charles William de la Poer Beresford had the unusual distinction of serving as an MP whilst a Royal Naval Officer. The Borough Council had agreed to award him the Honorary Freedom of the Borough in recognition of 'his uniform consideration of the Borough whilst in charge of the fleet' during his service at Portland from 1907 to 1909. Preparations were authorised for an appropriate ceremony 'at a cost not exceeding £20'. The ceremony took place on Tuesday 12 May 1914 at the Pavilion, the programme for the event stating, 'Councillor Mr Warwick will kindly sing *Rule Britannia* and the audience are requested to join in the chorus'. Alderman Templeman paid for the cost of the entertainment.

Motor racing organised by the Dorset Automobile Club on Saturday 7 June 1913 on Weymouth sands. A contemporary account refers to dozens of cars flying over the beach close to the water's edge at speeds averaging nearly sixty miles per hour.

A memorial to Weymouth-born sixteenth-century navigator Richard Clark, and colleague John Endicott, who sailed from Weymouth in 1628, was unveiled by Mrs Joseph Chamberlain, one of Endicott's descendants, on Tuesday 2 June 1914. It stood in front of the old Pavilion Theatre until it was removed to the Alexandra Gardens in the mid-1950s following the Ritz fire. Following representations from the Weymouth Civic Society it was moved to a location at Ferry Steps in 2003.

The cessation of hostilities which marked the end of the First World War is greeted by crowds on 12 November 1918 at the King's Statue. The street scene shows many service personnel present, along with residents.

A postcard that shows an Armistice Day thanksgiving after the First World War.

On Tuesday 24 June 1924 a Westland Walrus plane of the Fleet Air Arm took off from Chickerell airfield with three crew members. Shortly after take off one of the wheels fell off and the crew decided to bring the plane down in Weymouth Bay. Here the rescue boats are in attendance and an interested crowd looks on.

A Royal Naval wedding procession on the Esplanade passing the Jubilee Clock in 1920. Note the hedges along the Esplanade. A horse cabman watches with interest whilst another horse with its owner also waits to get by. On the balcony of the houses some ladies are also watching. The sailors are actually pulling the vehicle which contains the bridegroom.

In July 1923 the Prince of Wales (the future King Edward VIII) visited Weymouth and Dorchester and is seen returning to Weymouth Railway Station accompanied by the Mayor, Cllr W.J. Gregory, in time to catch the 5.20 p.m. train. The crowd control appears to have been extremely effective as none is visible! The building is adorned with enamel signs advertising Pears Soap, Player's Navy Mixture tobacco and other products. Such signs today are highly prized by collectors!

Crowd scenes on the Esplanade earlier that day. Well-wishers surround the car.

The Duke of York (later King George VI) formally opened the Town Bridge on Friday 4 July 1930. Following a procession from the King's Statue, the Duke operated the machinery to raise the bridge and Cosens and Company's paddle steamer *Empress* with school children on board passed through the bridge from the Backwater.

Sailors returning from leave in 1912. A cargo has been unloaded from the Channel Islands steamer. Caught up in the mêlée are two carts belonging to Drake & Sons, a local fruit and vegetable wholesalers, possibly collecting vegetables from the Channel Islands. The sailors are waiting to catch the steamer to take them back to Portland.

five

Ships and Transport

:: LIST OF ::
BATTLESHIPS, CRUISERS
&c.

Published by EDWIN H. SEWARD,
13, TURTON STREET, WEYMOUTH.

In the "MELCOMBE SERIES" of Real Photo Post Cards.

OBTAINABLE AT ALL ENTERPRISING STATIONERS.

PRICE 2d. EACH:
ALSO ENLARGEMENTS AND LANTERN SLIDES.

Aboukir	Doris	Kangaroo	Sutlej
Achilles	Duke of Edinburgh	Kestrel	Swift
Acteon	Duncan	King Edward VII.	Swiftsure
Adventure	Drake	Leander	Talbot
Africa	Dreadnought	Leda	Temeraire
Agamemnon	Eclipse	Liffey	Thorn
Albemarle	Edgar	Lightning	Topaze
Amethyst	Enchantress	Liverpool	Triumph
Andromeda	Essex	London	Tyne
Antrim	Euryalus	Lord Nelson	Vanguard
Argonaut	Exmouth	Magnificent	Venerable
Arrogant	Express	Maine	Vengeance
Arun	Falmouth	Majestic	Victoria and Albert
Aquarius	Fawn	Mars	Victorious
Assistance	Ferret	Minotaur	Vigilant
Bedford	Formidable	Monmouth	Warrior
Bellerophon	Forward	Moy	Waveney
Prince	Garry	Natal	Wizard
Blenheim	Glasgow	New Zealand	
Blonde	Glory	Neptune	Home Fleet at Anchor
Boyne	Gloucester	Nubian	Home Fleet Illuminated
Bristol	Goliath	Ocean	Prayers at Sea
Britannia	Good Hope	Ostrich	Sailors Going on Leave
Bulwark	Gossamer	Pathfinder	Sailors Returning from Leave
Cæsar	Greyhound	Patrol	Serving out Grog
Canopus	Halcyon	Peterel	Towing Targets
Carnarvon	Hampshire	Petroleum	Testing Cables, Etc., Etc.
Charger	Hannibal	Prince George	
Cochrane	Harrier	Recruit	United States Warships
Collingwood	Hecla	Renown	Connecticut
Colne	Hercules	Revenge	Delaware
Commonwealth	Hibernia	Ribble	Itasca
Cornwall	Hindustan	Rocket	Kansas
Cressy	Hogue	Roebuck	Louisiana
Cumberland	Illustrious	Roxburgh	Michigan
Cyclops	Imperieuse	Royal Arthur	North Dakota
Cygnet	Irresistible	Russell	South Carolina
Colossus	Isis	Ruby	New Hampshire
Defence	Itchen	Sapphire	
Derwent	Indefatigable	Seagull	Italian—
Devonshire	Indomitable	Sentinel	San Marco
Diamond	Inflexible	Shannon	
Dido	Invincible	Skirmisher	Turkish—
Dominion	Implacable	St. Vincent	Hamadieh
Donegal	Juno	Suffolk	
Doon	Jupiter	Superb	Japanese—
	Kale	Surprise	Kurama
			Tone

Seward's postcards feature many of the ships of the Royal and foreign navies which visited Portland. This is an advertisement for such postcards – note the fact that they are obtainable at all enterprising stationers!

Visits from the fleet were of constant interest, even more so when illuminated displays were given. Seward has photographed the illuminated vessels in Portland Roads giving an impressive illustration of the might of the British Navy at the time.

HMS *Weymouth*, seen here off Bincleaves, was a light cruiser launched in 1911. A fine silver table centrepiece made by John Vincent, the Weymouth jeweller was presented to the captain as a gift from the inhabitants, the cost being raised by public subscription initiated by Councillor R.C. Watts, who himself made a generous contribution. Following the vessel's withdrawal the silverware was displayed in a number of Royal Naval establishments throughout the world but returned to HMS *Osprey*, Portland, in 1983. In 1998, following the closure of HMS *Osprey*, the Royal Navy presented the silverware to the borough council on permanent loan where it can be seen on display at the council offices.

HMS *Titania*, submarine depot ship with a number of submarines alongside. This vessel was built in 1915 and served in China and Hong Kong. She served at Portland from 1930 to 1939 and was broken up in 1948.

Royal Yacht *Victoria and Albert* was a frequent visitor to Weymouth in her long career from 1893 to 1952. She frequently attended naval reviews and in this photograph the other ships are dressed overall.

HMS *Royal Oak*, a battleship of the Royal Sovereign class, was built at Devonport between 1914 and 1916. She was present at the Review of the Home Fleet by King George VI in Weymouth Bay in 1938 but became an early casualty of the Second World War, being torpedoed by a U-boat in Scapa Flow in October 1939 with the loss of 833 members of her crew.

HMS *Rodney*, a battleship of the Nelson class, was designed as a battle cruiser of 48,000 tons. However, the Washington Treaty of 1922 imposed a limit of 35,000 tons on all capital ships and her total length was reduced by 200ft, giving her a curious sawn off appearance. She was present at fleet reviews at Weymouth in 1932 and 1938. She served throughout the Second World War with distinction and took a prominent part in the action against the *Bismarck* in May 1941. She was placed in reserve in 1945 and scrapped in 1948.

Disembarking troops at Weymouth in 1919 is the paddle steamer *Mona's Queen* of the Isle of Man Steam Packet Company. Painted in camouflage to distract enemy gun sights, she had served as a troopship since 1915. Her most notable achievement was the sinking of an enemy submarine.

The Austrian freighter *Kostrena* was captured by British warships in 1914 and held in Weymouth harbour during the first few weeks of the First World War. Following her release she was interned in Vigo, Spain. After the First World War she was sold firstly to an Italian company and then to Yugoslavia. In 1941 she was taken over by the Ministry of War Transport and renamed the *Radfield*. In 1947 she was again renamed *Tuzla*, under Yugoslavian control, and was broken up in 1953, fifty-one years after her launching in Glasgow.

The Blue Funnel line steamer *Patroclus* struck the rocks at Westcliff in 1907. She was sailing from Brisbane with a cargo of wool and skins when she ran ashore at Blacknor Point on Friday 13 September 1907. She was eventually refloated nine days later with the help of four tugs and a salvage vessel with eleven steam pumps working on deck. She returned to service after repair in Portland Harbour. She was sunk during the First World War.

The *Madeleine Tristan* loaded with grain from France was driven ashore in Chesil Cove on Saturday 20 September 1930. She gradually broke up over the following years. In 1931 it was reported in the local press that residents had found means of boarding the vessel over the bank holiday weekend 'experiencing the thrills of being on a real wreck'.

The *Preveza* was not as fortunate as the *Patroclus*. In June 1920 the Greek-owned vessel collected coal and stores at Portland which were not paid for before she left for Cardiff. She was refused entry there as she was not insured. Unfortunately for the owners and crew, whilst returning to Rotterdam she went aground broadside on Chesil. Local creditors nailed writs to the mast to prevent her from leaving. Heavy seas did their worst and she broke up.

The *Bulow*, a German liner stranded in fog at Mutton Cove on Sunday 14 June 1914 whilst on route between Yokohama and Southampton. The passengers continued their journey by train and the vessel was successfully refloated.

An interesting sight for residents out for a Christmas Day stroll in 1930 was the French ketch *L'Arguenon* aground on Weymouth beach. She was en route from Poole to St Malo and dropped her anchors on a windy night. Attempts by a naval steam pinnace to refloat her failed the following day and after lightening her ballast and with improvements in weather conditions she was towed off by Louis Basso, a well-known local salvage expert.

The paddle steamer *Majestic*, the largest steamer in Messrs Cosens' fleet, steaming out of Weymouth Harbour in around 1910. Built in 1901 for long-distance excursions this superb vessel became a war casualty in 1916 in the Mediterranean.

The paddle steamer *Emperor of India* seen departing from Weymouth Pier. This vessel was built in 1906 and purchased by Messrs Cosens two years later. She was subject to a number of rebuilds over the years and, although not as popular as some of the rest of the fleet, lasted until 1957. The large number of warships in the background proclaims the might of the British fleet before the First World War.

The paddle steamer *Monarch* backing away from Weymouth Pier before 1913, transporting sailors to Portland. She was built in 1888, served in both World Wars, and was finally broken up in 1950. In the background one of the GWR Lynx class Channel Island steamers is also leaving port.

The paddle steamer *Melcombe Regis* approaching Weymouth Pier during the summer of 1914. Built in 1902 as the *Lune* she was purchased and renamed by Messrs Cosens in 1913 to assist with their naval contracts. In the background Weymouth's stone pier is being lengthened and the fleet are gathering in preparation for the hostilities that were threatening Europe. A steam launch, looking somewhat overloaded, follows the paddle steamer into the harbour.

One of the favourite short excursions by steamer from Weymouth was to Lulworth Cove. The paddle steamer *Victoria* seen in the Cove is unloading passengers over the bow gangway. The *Victoria* was broken up in 1952 although this type of cruise continued with successor vessels owned by Cosens until 1963. On the shore a 'refreshment trolley', which looks somewhat unstable, prepares to feed passengers and one can only marvel at the impracticability of the dresses of the ladies who were on the vessel.

Upwey Wishing Well Halt, with a local train departing for Weymouth. Whilst there were three stations with Upwey in their name none of them were in the parish of Upwey. Two of the stations – Upwey Wishing Well Halt and Upwey Junction – were on the main line to London. Note the vast tract of undeveloped land between Upwey and the sea – a very different picture greets the railway passenger looking out from the train today with the Weymouth Relief Road running alongside the line.

Upwey Junction in 1926 looking towards Dorchester with a down train from Bournemouth approaching. To the left the single track of the branch to Abbotsbury, opened in November 1885, can be seen. The branch line closed in November 1952. The junction was later renamed Upwey and Broadwey but is now called Upwey – a halt serving the north part of Weymouth.

Upwey Station on the Abbotsbury branch line in the 1920s. Despite its rural appearance with the milk churns on the platform this station was but a short distance from the main road to Dorchester. At one stage a railway camping coach which provided affordable holidays was located here. To the right, in the goods yard, railway coal wagons are standing.

A pre-1914 view of Rodwell Station on the Weymouth–Portland branch shown after its reconstruction with a passing loop during 1907. A GWR saddle tank awaits departure with a Weymouth-bound train. Posters on the station advertise excursions to Swanage. To the left of the station flower plots can be seen and the station was a frequent winner in the Best Kept Station competition. Although not visible in the photograph, a greenhouse was situated on the platform which no doubt helped the station's success. These flowerbeds lasted until the Second World War when they were used for vegetable cultivation when station staff bred rabbits to help eke out the meat rations!

A snowy day on the down platform of Radipole Halt in 1909. The station opened in 1905 as a move against proposed tram services within the borough. In the background is the Spa Hotel built in 1899 to replace the old Pig and Whistle which was situated on the opposite corner of Spa Road.

A GWR 850 class 0-6-0ST locomotive waits to depart from the newly opened Melcombe Regis station with a Portland train during 1909. Over the years infilling of Radipole Lake has changed the scene. Today the King's Roundabout and retail buildings occupy this site.

Great Western Railway 517 class 0-4-2 tank number 524 stands at Abbotsbury Station having arrived with a branch train from Weymouth. On the platform stand milk churns and baskets used to convey rabbits to poultry merchants. The sender of the card enquires of the recipient, (a resident of Abbotsbury), 'do you know any of the gentlemen on the other side?'

An unidentified road accident at a place unknown. A lorry loaded with pipes has come to grief. A marine boiler is also involved and a traffic jam has built up. A number of people have gathered offering advice — what were their suggestions as to the cause?

Other local titles published by The History Press

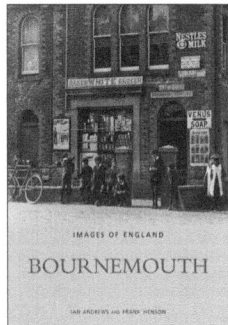

Bournemouth
IAN ANDREWS AND FRANK HENSON

This collection of 200 archive images traces some of the changes and developments that have taken place in the seaside town of Bournemouth during the last century. Pictures include schools and churches, shops and businesses – including Marshall & Bower the builders on Elmes Road and switchboard employees at the GPO Telephone Private Exchange at The Royal Bath Hotel in the 1920s – to sporting events and local townspeople.
07524 3065 3

Around Bridport and Lyme Regis
GERALD GOSLING AND LES BERRY

This book documents the history of the two harbour towns of Bridport and Lyme Regis, and looks at the histories of many of the villages around this area, including Charmouth, Marshwood, Stoke Abbott, Broadwindsor, Beaminster, Netherbury and Melplash. This volume illustrates these community histories with over 100 old photographs, which capture the essence of the area's rural heritage and its shipping industry.
07524 3074 2

Historic Gardens of Dorset
TIMOTHY MOWL

Until 1900 Dorset remained the semi-feudal society that Thomas Hardy knew, and its gardens reflected that. Small manor houses of the sixteenth and seventeenth centuries lay tucked away in downland folds or by winterbourne meadows. Then, in the late twentieth century, a new wave of designers settled in the county creating the historic gardens of the future. This book will set readers driving off to make their own judgements in our last unspoilt Arcadian county.
07524 2535 8

In Dorset's Skies
COLIN CRUDDAS

Dorset, a county of outstanding natural beauty, can rightly lay claim to another exceptional feature – its aeronautical heritage. Included are views of the rich aviation heritage of the county from those pioneer days of 1910 when the first purpose-built airfield in the county was opened for the Bournemouth International Aviation Meeting (one of the first in Britain), through two world wars, the post-war use of Tarrant Rushton as a base for Flight Refuelling Ltd and the developments that have led to the expansion of Bournemouth International.
07524 1734 7

If you are interested in purchasing other books published by The History Press, or in case you have difficulty finding any of our books in your local bookshop, you can also place orders directly through our website
www.thehistorypress.co.uk